SAMSUNG GALAXY S10e

Manual for Beginners

Best SAMSUNG S10 SERIES USER GUIDE with troubleshooting tips for seniors

MARY C. HAMILTON

Copyright© 2019

All rights reserved

No part of this book shall be reproduced, edited and transmitted without the prior notice of the author and publishers.

Dedicated

To

        John

        Mark

        Luke

        Natasha

I love you all

Acknowledgment

I want to thank my colleagues at *TechVerse* for their support and contributions in making this work a success.

Table of Contents

Preface 9

SECTION 1 11

INTRODUCTION TO GALAXY S10 SERIES
.... 11

    What's new 15

SECTION 2 20

THE SETUP 20

    How to set up your Samsung Galaxy S10e, S10 & S10 Plus 21

    Choose your Galaxy language 23

    Register fingers on Galaxy S10 sensor scanner 28

    Making Samsung Galaxy S10 your own . 32

Customize your Galaxy S10 screen display 34

How to customize Galaxy S10 Edge Panel 35

How to Customize ring tone on Galaxy S10 36

Remap the Bixby button on Galaxy S10 . 38

How to set up mobile data tracking on Galaxy S10 40

SECTION 3 43

USING THE SAMSUNG CAMERA 43

How to manage Galaxy S10 front camera punch holes 44

Samsung Galaxy S10 HDR10+ Display advantage 47

A look at Galaxy S10 cameras 50

SECTION 4 55

OTHER EXCITING TIPS AND TRICKS ... 55

How to set up Secure Folder 56

Set up your Samsung Galaxy Backup 59

Enable Find My Samsung Mobile 62

How to transfer data from your old phone to Galaxy S10 series 65

How to set up the Night Mode on Galaxy S10 series 71

How to minimize home screen grid size .. 74

How to lock down your Samsung S10 app layout 76

How to adjust font size & style on Samsung Galaxy S10 78

Restoring Samsung Galaxy S10 Always On Display 81

Restore vivid color on Samsung Galaxy S10 83

Tweak your Samsung Galaxy S10 Quick Settings Panel 85

SECTION 5 89

HOW TO TROUBLESHOOT COMMON
GALAXY S10 PROBLEMS 89

DISCLAIMER 95

ABOUT THE AUTHOR 96

Preface

It has been observed that nowadays people only purchase high end phones because of the prestige that comes with it. I can arguably say that more than 60 percent of high end phone users do not utilize their device to its maximum capacity. The Samsung Galaxy S10 is a perfect example of such device.

This trend would likely continue or even get worse due to the bloom in technology and the whole added features in recently released phones.

However, to avoid the possibility of such situation, the author has taken it upon herself to write this book for users of the S10 devices to utilize every feature of their phones, from normal daily to day routinely usage to advanced specific functions.

Sit back, relax and become a pro user of your S10 device in just a single read. If your phone is handy, follow along as the author takes you through a very smooth ride using your personal device.

SECTION 1

INTRODUCTION TO GALAXY S10 SERIES

Each year, leading smartphone makers revise and update their flagship models. They've done so for a whole decade, and you can easily tell why they do it.

First, the tech world is in the state of flux, changing by the hour. Tech engineers and researchers look for better, faster and safer way of doing things. Their effort do yield results in the form of devices with improved security features, ones that are easier to use, or more friendly with the environment.

The second and most important reason for periodic tech update and remodeling is the profit motive. Smartphone makers are in the business to make money for their stakeholders. The only way to keep making money is to keep selling their products.

Fact is, sales of any particular model tends to taper off within months of its unveiling. So, the only way for producers to keep up sales and meet sales targets is to render existing models obsolete, by redesigning and updating them every now and then.

This has been the tradition of *Samsung Electronics of South Korea*, and their competitors. Samsung rolled out a sensational Galaxy S smartphone in 2010. Since then, it has issued new versions of the S-line each year.

The Samsung Galaxy S10 series, released in 2019, corresponds with the 10th anniversary of the S-line premium smartphone. Samsung Company did not disappoint its customers around the world who trust them to always come up with exciting smartphone innovations year in, year out.

What's new

Each time a new version appears, you're curious to know what has really changed. Also, you'd want to determine if the changes are significant enough to warrant your incurring additional cost, especially when the previous model you owned is barely one year old, and still performing to your satisfaction.

In Galaxy S10 siblings --- the S10e, S10 baseline & upmarket S10 Plus --- you're sure to find significant innovations to justify your decision to migrate to the latest version, if you've not done so already.

Samsung Galaxy S10 parades these key features:

- *Android 9.0 Pie, One UI 8GB Random Access Memory (RAM)*

- *6.1 inches (15.4 cm) Dynamic active matrix organic light emitting diode (AMOLED) capacitive Touchscreen, 1440 x 3040 pixels*

- *HDR10 Always On Display*

- *Octa-core Qualcomm Snapdragon 845 CPU for products available in USA, Latin America and China. And Octa-core Exynos 9810 for Europe and the rest of the world.*

- *HDD store space of 128GB to 512GB, up to 1TB for S10+, all with additional Solid State Drive (SSD) card up to 512GB*

- *Three rear cameras 12MP wide, 12MP ultra-wide and 16MP telephoto & 10MP front camera for ultimate selfie*

- *Ultra-sonic, high sensitive Fingerprint scanner under Display*

- *Optimized wireless charging*

- *Water & dust proof IP68 compliant*

- *Non-removable 3,400mAh (4,100mAh for upmarket S10+) Li-ion battery capable of going 12 hours 35 minutes on a single charge.*

The bare skeleton, as bulleted above, may not tell all the story about the goodness of your Galaxy S10 series. So, we'll go ahead to flesh up things a bit.

In the S10, you get an all screen, near-zero bezel design. This means that nearly all the front of the device is touchscreen, giving you an impression of edge-to-edge Display, a virtual Infinity.

Samsung is on record to have produced the tiniest bezel ever known in the smartphone world. The near elimination of bezel in the S10 gives you larger screen without increasing the overall size of the phone. It's got much wider screen estate while measuring only 2 millimeters taller and wider than the preceding S9 series.

The endless front screen is, however, interrupted by the placement of the front camera inside an O-shaped cutout, top right of the screen. This explains the Infinity-O alias, by which the phone is called.

SECTION 2

THE SETUP

How to set up your Samsung Galaxy S10e, S10 & S10 Plus

Now, let's assume you've got the latest Sammy in town, any of the 2019 Galaxy S10 siblings. There are a few things that should be uppermost in your mind. One of them is how to properly set up your device so you can derive optimum user experience from it.

It's tempting to ignore everything else and start exploring and putting it to use immediately. But you'd agree with me that it's much wiser to spend a few moments to customize the device and make it truly yours.

It's not only a matter of inserting your SIM card and plugging to a wall power source for full juice. You've got to **switch on the device** and go through the entire **set-up** procedure so your device could resume working at its best.

Okay, you may have used Sammy Galaxy flagships, especially from S8 and S9 models. So, the set up process shouldn't be new, or hard. You already know how to **select the language, adjust the date and so forth.** Let's go over language selection for the benefit of users **who're new** to the Sammy family.

Choose your Galaxy language

If English is the only language you speak, you may not need to do anything about language selection, except to choose between American and British variations. But if you use any other tongue beside English, or you're polyglot and would like to alternate between languages, you've got to select the additional languages in the **General Management view** of the **Settings app.** It's also here that you choose either American or British English.

You'd be delighted to know that your Sammy 10 supports close to 12 key world languages, including the ubiquitous English (American/British variants) Spanish, German, French, Chinese, Korean, Italian and others. Regional variations of the key tongues are also supported.

When you choose one language, your Galaxy S10 immediately applies it to all its features **like menus, dialog boxes, screens, including native and third party apps.**

If you speak more than one language, of course, you can add all of them, and switch among them, as your mood or circumstances move you.

This is how you **Add languages** to your Galaxy S10:

- Go to **Settings**
- Choose **General Management**
- Select **Language & input**
- Tap **Language**
- With English as default language, choose **Add Language**

From nearly a dozen options, tap on the language you want to add. Select the regional variations of the language you want. A pop-up will let you set the language of your choice as default tongue. All the features in the phone will reflect your chosen language.

Let's assume you're through with language selection, date adjustment and signing in to your Google account. You've also connected the device to Wi-Fi network. It's time to **set up your biometric** authentication system, like the fingerprint recognition.

As you're aware, the fingerprint is used to gain access to your device. It's a lot easier to unlock your Galaxy S10 with the tip of your finger, than to draw complex patterns, or input your strong password, every now and then.

Though there was an initial problem with fingerprinting access method on the S10, Samsung acted quickly to rectify things. You can be sure now that no other finger can unlock your dear Sammy, to gain illegal entry to your digital secrets.

Register fingers on Galaxy S10 sensor scanner

- Swipe up or down on the Home screen to access the apps screen

- Select **Settings**

- Choose **Biometrics & Security**

- On Biometrics, tap **Fingerprints**. You may be asked to enter your PIN, input a password or draw pattern to continue

- Then choose **Continue** when the bar shows up

- Swipe your fingertip over S10 scanner to register

- Tap **Done** when the process is completed

- Hit the **Fingerprint unlock switch** to either open or shut down your device.

You have options to **add or remove saved fingerprints.** As you choose, remember that the sensor scanner may refuse to work if your hands are dirty, wet, oily or dyed.

Still in the set up phase, you may need to **download software updates** immediately so your device would start off in the best possible condition. Do not think that, because your Galaxy S10 is brand new, everything in it is up to date. Truth is, software updates can be available a day after the release of any particular model.

In the particular case of Galaxy S10 series, a couple of weeks after their launch, it was discovered that a thin film of screen protector could fool the ultrasound fingerprint scanner, such that anybody can unlock the phone. Within a week, Samsung Electronics worked hard to push out software to correct the problem.

Truth is, if you take time to walk through the set up process for your smartphone from the onset, and check out the latest software updates, you'd find it easier than seeking out the set up items later. Also, starting off with everything properly set up and updated, would help your device resume work in optimum condition.

Making Samsung Galaxy S10 your own

Part of what you achieve in the set up stage is to customize your device to suit your needs and tastes. If you chose to import your digital wealth from your previous smartphone (strongly recommended as part of the set up process) all your apps in the old phone will download automatically into your new device.

Otherwise, you hit Google Play Store to download the apps that you need to work or play around. You can choose to explore new apps, other than the ones you've always used.

There's no harm in exploring, or trying something new. You may just discover something you've been missing.

Customize your Galaxy S10 screen display

You've got a range of wallpapers to choose from. Of course, you can always change them according to your mood. Many use selfie, or photos of loved ones, as wallpaper. It's up to you.

If you intend to use the **Edge Panel**, you'll need to configure it, as part of your screen display set-up. It's a small bar at the right edge of the screen, where you can swipe to gain quick access to apps, contacts, mails or other features that you choose to have in the panel.

How to customize Galaxy S10 Edge Panel

- Go to **Settings**
- Select **Display**
- Scroll down to **Edge** screen and tap on it
- Select **Edge Panels**

Then choose the panels you wish to have on screen. It makes sense to have Contact among the items here.

How to Customize ring tone on Galaxy S10

At this point in your set up process, you'd like to choose your preferred sounds for calls, notifications and alarms. This is how to do that:

- Open to **Settings**
- Select **Sound & Vibration**
- Tap on **Ringtones**
- In the picker list that opens, tap the **+ sign** at top right
- From the sound picker app, select the ringtone or sound that thrills you.

That's the same way you choose your sounds for **alarms and notifications.** You may even wish to download a third party app, **Zedge**, to discover more sounds and tones that you can use.

Not forgetting that you can install a music file and take any of your favorite tunes from there to apply as your ringtone. Samsung gives you every opportunity to indulge yourself. It's called unlimited choice.

Remap the Bixby button on Galaxy S10

Your Galaxy S10 comes with a button dedicated to Bixby, Samsung's trademark digital voice assistant. It is located on the **upper left side** of the device. In case you have no need for Bixby voice assistance, you can remap its button to serve other purpose. For instance, you can redirect it to open any app of your choice, or run a command to turn on the Bluetooth.

To remap the Bixby button:

- Go to **Settings**

- Choose **Advanced Features**
- Select **Bixby key**, then assign new duty to the key

If you would rather use Google Assistant, you can't use Bixby key to launch it on Galaxy S10. It's been blocked from the factory by Samsung. Also, you can't completely disable Bixby. You can only assign new duty to its dedicated button.

Even when you remap it, a long press on the button will always bring back the virtual voice assistant.

How to set up mobile data tracking on Galaxy S10

If you enjoy unlimited data plan, you don't have to worry about tracking your data consumption. Otherwise, it's wise to monitor your usage to ensure you do not go beyond the limit of your subscription, with serious impact on the credit card balances.

This is how to monitor your data consumption:

- Go to **Settings**
- Select **Connections**
- Choose **Data Usage**

- Then, **Billing cycle & Data warning**

Here, you can fill in your billing cycle and the data limit obtainable in your plan. By enabling data warning feature, you get to be reminded when you're close to the danger zone.

Samsung Galaxy S10 comes with inbuilt data usage tracker. That should be okay for your need. But if, for whatever reason, you choose to do something different, you can download third party apps for data tracking.

My Data Manager, for instance, can be installed for free, from Google

Play Store. And it offers many exciting features.

SECTION 3

USING THE SAMSUNG CAMERA

How to manage Galaxy S10 front camera punch holes

Many have complained about the front camera punch holes. They can constitute an eyesore, especially when the app on display contains white background. While the S10e, and S10 both have a single punch hole for their sole front camera, the upscale S10 Plus parades two punch holes.

It's good to know that you can black out the intruding holes if they irritate you, as they do many users. You can hide the holes in any of the models, replacing it with a black bar.

Do it this way:

- Swipe from top of the screen downward
- Select **Settings**
- Tap **Display**
- Select **Full Screen apps**
- Toggle the Hide Front Camera button.

A black bar will appear in the place of the camera holes on your screen. It's your judgment call to make, if the black ribbon is more tolerable to you than the camera punch holes.

Again, you can determine which apps should display full screen, displacing the camera position with the bar, and which shouldn't.

Just locate the apps you do not want to go full screen, change their setting, **from full screen to auto.**

Samsung Galaxy S10 HDR10+ Display advantage

Another new feature of the Galaxy S10 series is the **HDR10 Plus**. It's been said in some circles, that the high dynamic range (HDR10 Plus) is one of the most significant innovations made by Samsung Electronics in the S10 devices. As you may know, every phone screen has a given range of colors that it can reproduce. That's what they call the dynamic range.

When we talk of high dynamic range plus, it refers to screens that reproduce over one billion color range. But, rather than set the range of colors on any particular number, the HDR10+, developed by Samsung, allows for continuous tweaking of the display settings so you can always see the best color possible.

The **HDR10+** feature, coupled with the active matrix organic light emitting diode (AMOLED), gives Samsung S10 devices their outstanding screen brilliance. It's a crisp view, near natural rendition that other phone makers would work hard to match.

Your S10 display is warmer than the preceding S9 premium. Samsung made conscious effort to reduce the AMOLED blue light level, so much so that Galaxy S10 is said to be 42 percent lower in blue light emission, than the S9 series.

The lower blue light is good news to all Sammy smartphone lovers. It's known to science that blue light is implicated in sleep distortion and eye pain that sometimes afflict heavy users of portable devices.

Lower blue light emission and better color display are good reasons to choose any of the Samsung Galaxy S10 siblings.

A look at Galaxy S10 cameras

In the preceding S9 series, Samsung Electronics thrilled consumers with dual back cameras that produced the *bokeh effect*, the ability of your lens to produce beautiful aesthetics even with out-of-focus background details.

In the 2019 updates, Samsung upped the ante with the introduction of one more rear camera, making a tri-camera content, of the following makes:

- Rear camera 1 is 12 megapixel, OIS (optical image

stabilization), double phase detection, instamatic & f/1.5 and f/2.4 apertures.

- Rear camera 2 is also 12MP, telephoto lens with f/22 aperture, dual optical zoom.

- Rear Camera 3, the new addition, is 16 megapixels, ultra-wide angle capable of shooting 4K videos at 60 frames per second.

Combined, the multi camera design enables you to capture a wider world with the dexterity of a pro. And guess what, using the cameras wouldn't give you any sweat.

When your phone is unlocked, the **camera icon** is there at the lower right corner of the screen. You can launch the app with a gentle tap on the icon. But from a locked screen, you can also tap on the icon, but drag it to the center to launch the camera.

Whether locked or open, you can mobilize your Galaxy S10 cameras by **double pressing the power button.** This quick launch should be on default. If not, you can enable it.

- Open **Settings** in the camera app
- Scroll to **Quick launch**
- Toggle the button

With the camera app open, a double press on the power button will see you switching from the rear cameras to the front one, and vice versa, after a selfie.

The last two shots you took will display by the lower right of the screen when the camera app is open. Tapping on the recent photos takes you straight to the photo gallery, where your previous shots are stored by default.

To view all the available modes in the camera apps, **swipe** your screen from right to left, with the phone in portrait mode. In landscape position, you'll have to swipe up or down to see the options.

Don't forget to use the same swiping, from bottom right, diagonally up to top left, when you want to engage your Galaxy S10 in **One-handed mode.** It's a simple way to put all your Home screen resources within reach of the fingers in one hand.

As for getting to master all the photo possibilities in your Galaxy S10, it will take time and practice. It's the same for everything else we want to get used to; time and practice ensure success. But you'll be rewarded with memorable shots if you put forth efforts to master the tricks.

SECTION 4

OTHER EXCITING TIPS AND TRICKS

How to set up Secure Folder

It's in the secure folder that you hide those digital files of yours that you'd not like prying eyes of others to see. It's an encrypted zone on your device for storing apps, videos, files and anything at all that you wouldn't want anyone else to see.

To create a Secure Folder, you need to have a **Samsung account**. In case you don't have that already, quickly go to *https://account.samsung.com/membership/intro* and create one.

You won't pay to register as a Samsung member. And there are many benefits of doing this, including easy access to online help when things go wrong with your Galaxy S10, or any other Samsung device.

The moment you're on Samsung website:

- Locate the **Secure Folder** in the apps drawer
- Launch it
- Sign in with the Samsung account you created, using any of the authentication methods like pattern, fingerprint, PIN of password.

That's it. You can start adding your private files to the folder. And how do you do that? It's easy.

When you open the folder, you'd see the menu at the top, with options to add files, add apps and lock. You also have options to edit apps so you can arrange things the way you want inside the Folder.

Set up your Samsung Galaxy Backup

This one great advantage of having your Sammy S10 properly set up before putting it to work. In the process, you'd have to sign into the Samsung account. You need to create one, if you don't have it already.

As a registered member, you can set up **Samsung Pay** for easy online transactions. You can download apps from Samsung Galaxy Store. And what's more, you can enjoy the reliable Samsung Cloud backup.

When backed up in the Samsung Cloud service, your Sammy S10 will be helped to stay ever updated, making it a notch easier for you to restore operating features like Settings, native apps and home screen outlook with a few gentle taps.

To ensure your Galaxy S10 is properly backed up in the Samsung Cloud, following these easy steps:

- Start from the **Settings** app page
- Select **Accounts & backup**
- Tap on **Samsung Cloud**

In the Cloud, tap on the **three dots** at the top right corner of the screen and choose **Settings.** Then, choose **Sync &**

auto backup settings. Carefully go through the information in the field to verify what is backed up. You have options to add what should be backed up in Cloud and remove what you consider unworthy of this service.

Enable Find My Samsung Mobile

Agreed, you do not lose smartphones very frequently. Few adults do so. That's not to say that it doesn't ever happen that people leave their portable devices in cabs or at the clubs.

If you ever suffer the emotional pains of losing your dear Sammy Galaxy S10 in any circumstance, you'd wish you had enabled the **Find My Mobile** feature in your phone. Why not set up this important service as part of your start up. Or even do it now, if you've been using the S10 for a while, but never thought of what would you happen if your phone gets lost.

- As usual, proceed to the **Settings** app page
- Select Biometrics & Security
- Choose Find My Mobile

In the page, you'd have to adjust the settings to suit your needs. You may wish to enable **send the last known location** feature. If your phone is lost, you'll get to know where the phone was when it lost power.

If the need arises, all you need to do is go **to** *findmymobile.samsung.com* and sign in with your Samsung account and, pronto, you'll be able to track down your device. You'll be able to control its usage until you're able to locate it.

How to transfer data from your old phone to Galaxy S10 series

Another immediate need would be how to transfer your prized data from your old device to the new acquisition. Gladly, there are two ways you can do this, and both of them are easy and recommended by Samsung Electronics.

First, you can go through the **Smart Switch**. It's the official way Samsung wants you to move files among their portable devices. And it's good you adhere to this method to avoid endangering your digital assets.

If you own one of the older S-line devices, say Galaxy S6 and below, or you're using a device other than a smart Sammy, you'd need to install the **Smart Switch** app. Search it out on **Google Play Store.**

If you own the S7 and the versions after that, is pre-installed in them. With this app safely in your arsenal, you can move ahead to the next phase of moving your data to S10.

- Open the **Smart Switch** app on your new Galaxy S10
- Choose **Wireless**, then **Receive**
- Then select your old phone
- On the old phone, also select **Wireless**, then **Send**

- Then **Connect**. The two devices should connect automatically.

But you're not done yet. The process of transferring your digital wealth in the old phone has just begun, but on the right note.

Now that you've connected the two devices, wirelessly, choose the files you'll like to transfer from the old device.

- Then tap **Send** at the lower part of your screen
- Hold on a moment, as the file finishes its movement
- Tap **Finish** to conclude.

Apply the same method to other files until you're done moving everything of value from the old device.

Remember to completely remove everything that bears your imprints in the old phone, before selling it off, trading it in, gifting it or throwing it away.

Transferring data from old phones to Galaxy S10 through NFC

As we said earlier, there are two official methods for transferring data from old phones to the Galaxy S10 series. Let's quickly discuss the second route, through the **NFC** (Near Field Communication), a technology that allows wireless movement of data between two devices.

If your old phone has this capability, that is the NFC, you can use it to transfer data to your new Galaxy S10. Here's how you do it:

- Turn on the NFC features on both phones by going to **Settings**
- Choose **More Settings**
- Tap on **NFC**
- Link the two phones back to back.

You'd feel a vibration as confirmation that both are connected wirelessly and ready to share files. Your Wi-Fi must be turned on to enable electromagnetic induction to work between your two phones.

Choose the digital files you want to move. It could be your prized photos, contacts, music that's free from DRM protection, Word Document files, videos and S Notes. Happily, all these are NFC supported.

- When you choose a supported file on the old phone, tap **Transfer**
- Choose **Ok** to be sure that your action had been successful.

How to set up the Night Mode on Galaxy S10 series

It's better known as the **dark mode**. But Samsung Electronics prefer to call it Night Mode as if you're not allowed to use it in daytime. In reality, many Sammy S10 users just love the beauty of most apps in the Night Mode. And, it's not only about beauty. The dark mode extends battery life, in addition to being more lenient to your eyes.

Now, like every other thing you do on the Sammy premium phones, enabling the dark mode is simple. This is how you do it:

- Go to your phones **Settings** icon

- Scroll through menu options till you get to **Display**

- A tap on the Display will show you adaptive brightness, blue light filter etc.

- Select **Night Mode** toggle the button beside it.

The Night Mode is expected to be further optimized when Samsung finally rolls out its much publicized **Android 10-based One**

UI 2.0 update. Among other refinements, the One UI software overlay, taking the place of *Samsung Experience and TouchWiz,* will help Night Mode to switch on automatically at night fall.

You'll still retain the power to turn it on at any moment of the day, if you love the feel of it. Also, the One UI skin overlay will enhance one-handed use of most Sammy premium smartphones, starting from the 8th S-line and the Note 10 series.

How to minimize home screen grid size

There are times you wish to have more app icons displayed on your home screen. And you just feel a bit frustrated that the screen just can't take any more apps. Well, you can minimize the app grid so your phone can accommodate more app icons.

This is how you do it:

- Select a blank space on the home screen and long-press on it
- Tap Home screen settings
- From the options that show up, choose Home screen grid

- Proceed to adjust the grid size to your taste.

You're then able to accommodate more app icons on the home screen for easy access to the apps, or for the mere beauty of having the apps as decoration.

How to lock down your Samsung S10 app layout

As you resized your app grid and accommodated more app icons on the home screen, you also need to do something to hold them in place. It's often irritating to see app icons and widgets in disarray, just a few moments after you'd arranged them in a pleasant order.

It's up to you to lock down your home screen app layout in such a way that you'll not accidentally scatter things. And if you're a parent who allows children to watch videos or listen to favorite music on your S10 device, you can always expect them to rearrange your display icons without your permission. So, lock your app layout.

- Make a long press on any part of your home screen
- Choose **Home screen grid**
- Select **Lock Home screen layout**

You'll agree that everything you do on Galaxy S10 smartphone is as easy as ABC.

How to adjust font size & style on Samsung Galaxy S10

It's not the app grid size that you may wish to adjust. Sometimes, you'd feel like choosing a new typeface or resizing the very one you're currently using.

You can do it easily, this way:

- Start from **Settings**
- Choose **Display**
- Then, **screen zoom**
- From screen zoom, slide blue bar to the right or left, to

increase or decrease the font size.

One thing about Samsung S10 series is there are several ways of getting anything done on it.

- From the **Display**, you can choose **Font size & style** instead of zoom

- Then again, slide the blue bar right or left to resize your font

- In **font style** section, you find options to select a favorite typeface

The typeface you choose can be set as default, or just used for the work at hand.

Restoring Samsung Galaxy S10 Always On Display

You know how convenience it has always been to just glance at your smartphone and see time, date, battery percentage, pending notifications and everything else that you scheduled to be on display.

One thing you'll notice on Samsung Galaxy S10 with the introduction of One UI 2.0 is that the **Always on Display** mode isn't a default feature anymore. You've got to do something to wake up the display before you can enjoy the convenience of a quick time check and so on.

The good news is that Samsung gives you the liberty to restore the **Always On Display** feature on Galaxy S10, if that is what you like.

- Start from **Settings**
- Choose **Lock screen**
- Select **Always on display**
- Tap on **Show always**

You can determine the features you'd like to have on display, that is, in addition to time, date, notifications and battery juice level.

Restore vivid color on Samsung Galaxy S10

All of the S10 siblings are defaulted to natural look display out of the box. Samsung formerly set their devices on vivid color from the factory, so that users can adjust to natural tone if they so desire.

In case you find the natural look too muted for your liking, you can proceed to restore the vivid display.

- As always, go to **Settings**
- Choose **Display**
- Select **Screen Mode**

- Choose **Vivid** to replace the natural look

There are other options to customize your display color temperatures, and all of it can be accomplished in the **settings app display** page. You can adjust the brightness slider manually to suit various lighting conditions.

Tweak your Samsung Galaxy S10 Quick Settings Panel

Your Sammy **Quick Settings panel** is there on default and contains shortcuts for many important functions. But it's hardly ever organized the way you'd want. Also, the default appearance makes you scroll through several panes, leaving you to wonder just how quick the quick setting actually is.

Happily, you can refine things in the panel to suit your needs. Yes, you can rearrange the shortcuts and resize the grid to house more shortcuts.

- Swipe from the top of the screen until **Quick Setting Panel** fills the screen

- Tap over the 3-dot menu button

- Select **Button Grid**

- Choose the grid size that meets your need. The 5x3 options suits me.

Having resized your grid, you can use **Button order** option to rearrange the shortcut icons the way you like them to appear, bearing in mind that only the **first six** would be visible to you each time you view the pane.

Samsung Galaxy S10 also parades an adaptive brightness feature on default, which can remember your customized brightness setting under different light levels, and tweak the display accordingly when it encounters similar conditions.

There's also the inbuilt blue light filter that we previously mentioned as one of the significant innovations in the latest Sammy premium phone. You must surely turn this on at all times, to reduce blue light emission. Although particularly useful at night, the blue light filter can always help reduce eye strain at all times.

No manual of the sort you're now reading can possibly touch all you need to tweak on the Samsung Galaxy S10 to enhance your user experience. All that anyone could do is to get you off on the journey of endless discovery. We believe we have done so, that is, prepare you to explore the limitless world of the latest Samsung Electronics premium smartphone, the Galaxy S10 series.

SECTION 5

HOW TO TROUBLESHOOT COMMON GALAXY S10 PROBLEMS

From what's known about Galaxy S10 series, they are a great family of smartphones. Samsung Electronics of Korean has established itself as a trusted name in the industry. Yet, almost anything ever made by man can always misbehave without warning. As the saying goes, they just keep working until they disappoint.

There are many things that could go wrong with your darling S10. But many of the challenges are what you can fix by tweaking one or two things in the device.

Again, it is very much advisable that you sign up as member of worldwide

Samsung users' family. In the community, you can receive online support to fix nearly all the challenges that you may ever have as you enjoy the services of the Sammy flagship phone.

Galaxy S10 fingerprint sensor scanner problem

So, if your ultrasonic fingerprint scanner refuses to work well, check if your fingers are wet, dirty or greasy. Move your finger in different positions while holding the phone in one hand, of course. Remember that skin protectors can interfere with sensor scanner efficiency, despite software improvements to eliminate this.

How to prevent accidental S10 screen touch

To minimize accidental engagement of apps on the touch, due to infinity edge design of your S10, just;

- open the **Settings** app page,
- choose **Display**,
- Select **Accidental Touch protection** and switch it **On**.

Alternatively, you may want to disable the Edge apps pane completely. Since you enabled it yourself, it shouldn't hard for you to undo it.

Freezing and unresponsive S10 screen

It doesn't happen every time. But it can happen that your Galaxy S10 screen just freezes and refuses to obey command. It's not time for you to fret or contact Samsung Help Desk.

Many of the commonest problems you ever see on smartphones can be fixed by **shutting down**, and **rebooting your device.** Just try it on your Galaxy S10, and you're likely to see the screen responding again.

DISCLAIMER

All the hacks mentioned in this book have been subjected to various trials on different variants of the Samsung S10 device. They are sure to work perfectly well on your device.

However, the author and publishers would not be held accountable if any damage result when these tricks are not used appropriately.

Users should adhere strictly to instructions.

ABOUT THE AUTHOR

MARY HAMILTON is the CEO of *TechVerse,* a renowned software developing organization formed by tech gurus from around the world.

She is also a tech and gadget reviewer, who has written numerous "how-to" manuals for users to get to know their devices better.

Most of her books have been referenced by top magazines and tech websites as the gold standard for "User guides".

Enjoying her life in a small town in Texas, where she lives with her only daughter, Mary continues to write best seller books to help improve the tech world.